ARCTIC OCEAN

FRANZ JOSEF

SEVERNAYA ZEMLYA

NEW SIBERIAN ISLANDS

Wrangel Island

NOVAYA ZE

FINLAND

RUSSIA

ESTONIA

LATVIA

LITHUANIA

BELARUS

POLAND

UKRAINE

MOLDOVA

ROMANIA

BULGARIA

KAZAKHSTAN

MONGOLIA

GEORGIA

UZBEKISTAN

KRYGYSTAN

ARMENIA

AZERBAIJAN

TURKMENISTAN

TAJIKISTAN

GREECE

TURKEY

NORTH KOREA

NORTH PACIFIC OCEAN

MALTA

CYPRUS

LEBANON

SYRIA

IRAN

AFGHANISTAN

CHINA

SOUTH KOREA

JAPAN

PALESTINE

ISRAEL

JORDAN

IRAQ

KUWAIT

PAKISTAN

NEPAL

LIBYA

EGYPT

QATAR

UNITED ARAB EMIRATES

BANGLADESH

SAUDI ARABIA

OMAN

MYANMAR (BURMA)

LAOS

INDIA

CHAD

SUDAN

ERITREA

YEMEN

THAILAND

DJIBOUTI

VIETNAM

CAMBODIA

PHILIPPINES

GUAM

ADAMAN ISLANDS (INDIA)

ETHIOPIA

NICOBAR ISLANDS (INDIA)

FEDERATED STATES OF MICRONESIA

CENTRAL AFRICAN REPUBLIC

MARSHALL ISLANDS

SOMALIA

BRUNEI

MALDIVES

SRI LANKA

MALAYSIA

DEM. REP. OF THE CONGO

UGANDA

KENYA

RWANDA

KIRIBATI

BURUNDI

INDONESIA

PAPUA NEW GUINEA

SOLOMON ISLANDS

TANZANIA

SEYCHELLES

TUVALU

ANGOLA

MALAWI

COMOROS

SAMOA

ZAMBIA

VANUATU

FIJI

MOZAMBIQUE

MAURITIUS

TONGA

NAMIBIA

ZIMBABWE

NEW CALEDONIA (FRANCE)

BOTSWANA

MADAGASCAR

REUNION

INDIAN OCEAN

AUSTRALIA

SOUTH AFRICA

SWAZILAND

LESOTHO

NEW ZEALAND

TASMANIA (AUSTRALIA)

PRINCE EDWARD ISLANDS

ILES CROZET (FRANCE)

KERGUELEN ISLAND (FRANCE)

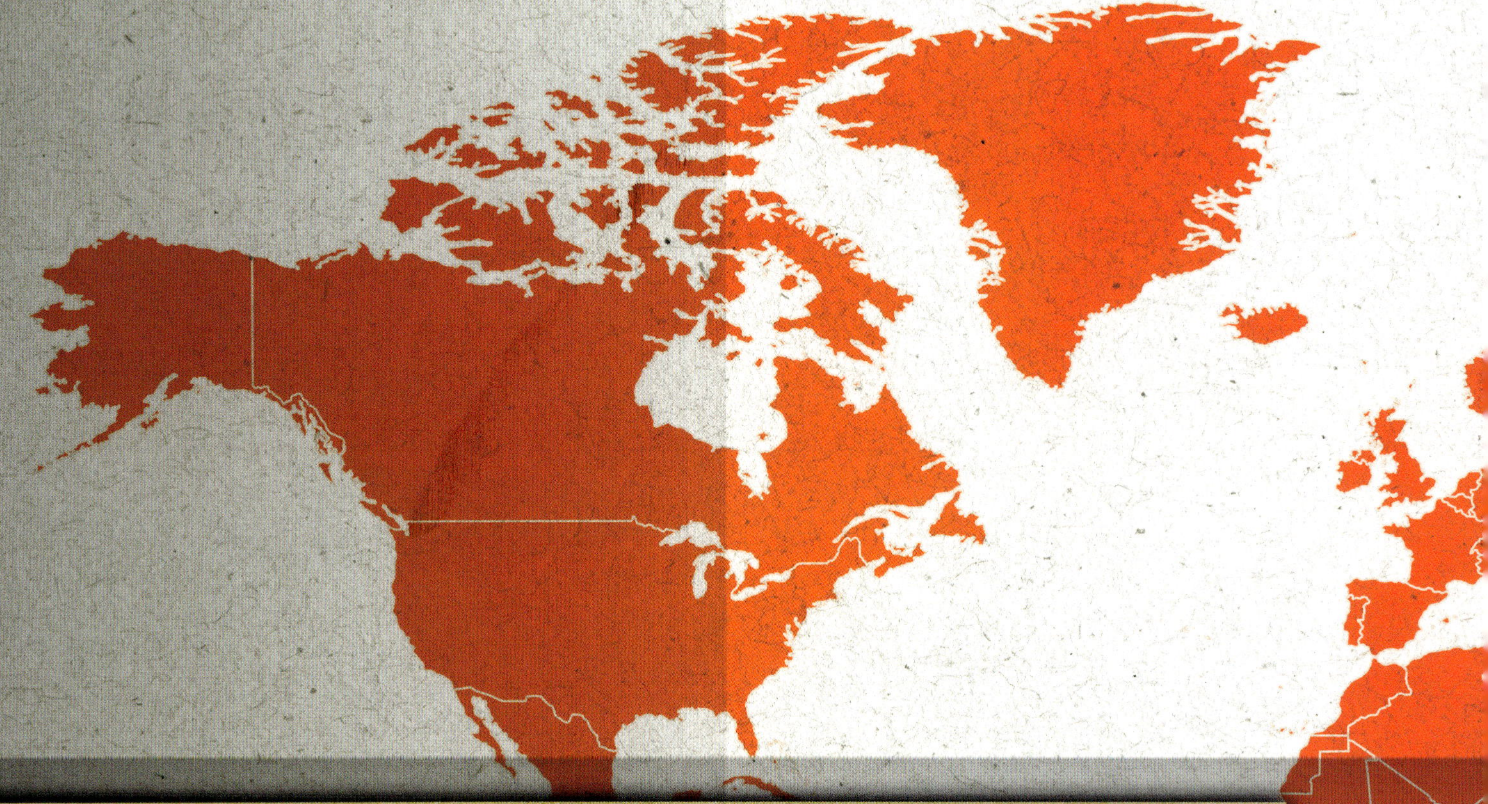

First Published 2022 by Redback Publishing
PO Box 357
Frenchs Forest NSW 2086
Australia

www.redbackpublishing.com
orders@redbackpublishing.com

ISBN 978-1-922322-40-1 HBK

Author: Jane Hinchey
Editor: Caroline Thomas
Design: Redback Publishing

Original illustrations © Redback Publishing 2022
Originated by Redback Publishing

Printed and bound in Malaysia

Acknowledgements
Abbreviations: l–left, r–right, b–bottom, t–top, c–centre, m–middle
We would like to thank the following for permission to reproduce photographs:
(Images © shutterstock) p4bl by Richie Chan, p4tr by Huy Thoai, p7br by thi, p8tl by Bule Sky Studio, p9tr by pradeep_kmpk14, DXLINH, p10bl CC BY-SA 3.0 <https://creativecommons.org/licenses/by-sa/3.0>, via Wikimedia Commons, p11mr by thi, p11br by Jimmy Tran, p12tr by Saigoneer, p13tr by Bob Pool, p13bl by Nina Lishchuk, p14tl by xuanhuongho, p16bl by Kobby Dagan, p17ml Saigoneer, p17br Public domain, via Wikimedia Commons (https://upload.wikimedia.org/wikipedia/commons/4/44/Hai_ba_trung_Dong_Ho_painting.jpg), p18tl by Yan_Liben, Public domain, via Wikimedia Commons, p18mr by SAS Scandinavian Airlines, Public domain, via Wikimedia Commons, p18bl Press and Information Office, Embassy of the Republic of Vietnam, Public domain, via Wikimedia Commons, p19tl The government-general of French Indo-China., Public domain, via Wikimedia Commons, p19mr, by artnana, p20tr, by pcruciatti, p20bl U.S. Marines in Japan Homepage, Public domain, via Wikimedia Commons, p20tr by Take Photo, p21tr by Huy Thoai, p21br by hecke61, p23tl by Ivan Kurmyshov, p26br by SARAH NGUYEN, p27tl by weltreisendertj, p28ml by Vietnam Stock Images, p28br by BREEZY STOCK, p29tr by British Library, CC0, via Wikimedia Commons, p29bl thi

A catalogue record for this book is available from the National Library of Australia

CONTENTS

MAP OF VIETNAM

Imperial City
HUE

Cu Chi Tunnels
HO CHI MINH CITY

Ho Chi Minh City
People's Committee Head Office

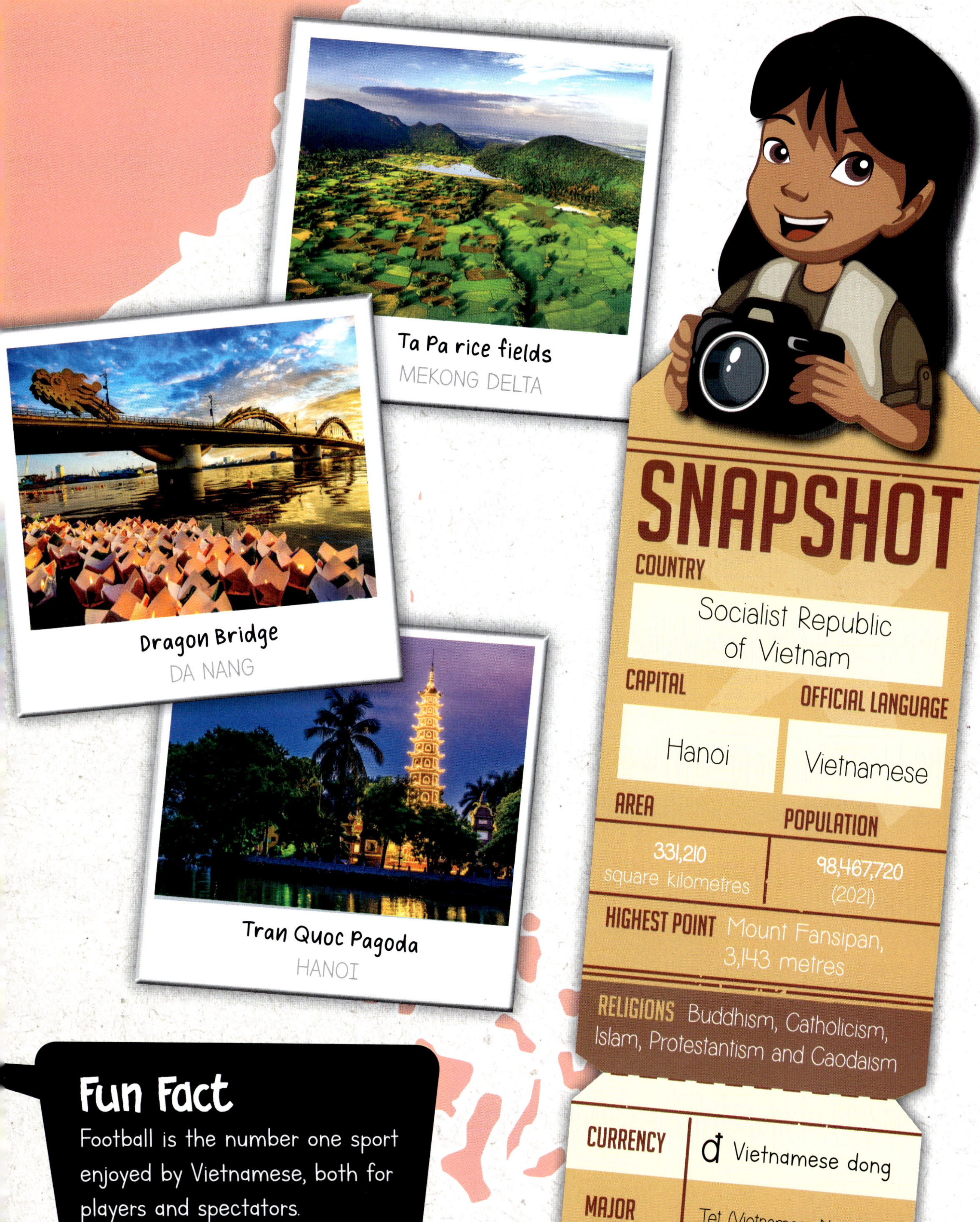

SNAPSHOT

COUNTRY
Socialist Republic of Vietnam

CAPITAL
Hanoi

OFFICIAL LANGUAGE
Vietnamese

AREA
331,210 square kilometres

POPULATION
98,467,720 (2021)

HIGHEST POINT Mount Fansipan, 3,143 metres

RELIGIONS Buddhism, Catholicism, Islam, Protestantism and Caodaism

CURRENCY đ Vietnamese dong

MAJOR FESTIVALS
Tet (Vietnamese New Year)
Vu Lan Festival (Day of Wandering Souls)
Mid-Autumn Festival

Fun Fact

Football is the number one sport enjoyed by Vietnamese, both for players and spectators.

WELCOME TO VIETNAM

The limestone sea rocks of Lan Ha Bay create around 300 tiny beaches

Vietnam is an 'S' shaped country in Southeast Asia. While not large, it is geographically diverse. It shares borders with Cambodia, Laos and the People's Republic of China. The body of water to the east is the South China Sea. The country has 3,260 kilometres of coastline, with the Gulf of Tonkin to the east and the Gulf of Thailand to the south. About 20 per cent of the country is level land, with the rest being tropical lowlands and densely forested highlands.

Terraced rice fields in Mu Cang Chai, Yen Bai

The Golden Bridge at Da Nang represents the hands of God offering gold from the land

The ancient village of Hoi An is a UNESCO National Cultural Heritage Site

Vietnam has enjoyed strong economic growth in recent years. Its main industries are rice, coffee, rubber, soybeans, seafood, sugarcane, cotton, tea and poultry. Tourism is now booming with travellers from all over the world visiting this beautiful, friendly country.

Empowering Women

There are many examples throughout Vietnamese history of female warriors. During the Vietnam War, women enlisted in the North Vietnamese Army (NVA) and worked for intelligence services.

Vietnamese teachers are highly valued by their students

Vietnamese women have many opportunities in education and work. They are prominent in the workforce and are entitled to paid maternity leave. Women play a prominent role in Vietnam's small-scale retail and trade markets, which include market stalls and shops. They also control the family budget.

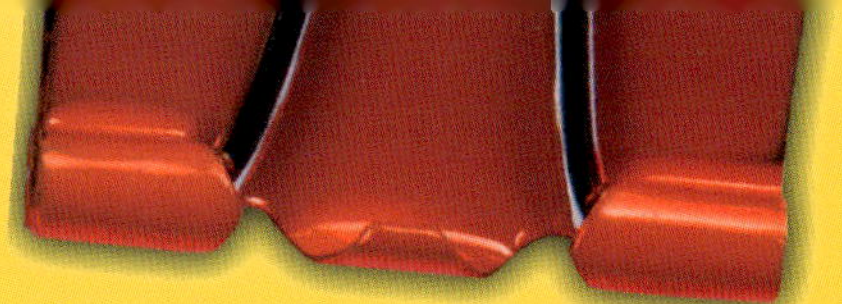

AT A GLANCE

Vietnam's government buildings have a statue of their first President, Ho Chi Minh

Government

Vietnam is a one-party socialist republic and the Communist Party is the only legal political party. The country is divided into 58 provinces and five municipalities.

Vietnam has a president, who is the head of state, elected by government members for a five-year term. The president appoints a prime minister, who leads the 26-member government.

Main Imports

Vietnam's main imports include electrical machinery, computer equipment, vehicles and medical instruments. Other imports include manufactured goods, raw materials for the shoe and textile industries, chemicals, fuels, food and live animals.

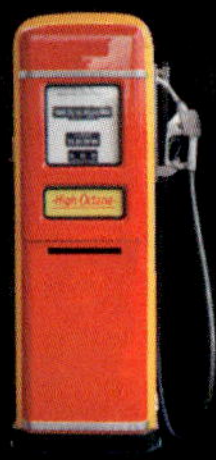

Main Exports

Vietnam's main exports are computers, petroleum, shoes, clothes, coffee and rice.

Natural Resources

Vietnam is rich in minerals and arable land and over 3,780 medicinal plant species grow there. Other natural resources include coal, manganese, offshore oil and gas, chromate and hydropower.

Salt farming is very profitable in Vietnam

Lotus seeds are used in Asian cuisine and traditional medicine

Áo dài

Traditional clothing in Vietnam includes a tunic over pants, called áo dài. Different cultural groups also have their own traditional clothing.

PEOPLE

Vietnam has a population of over 98 million people. While about 36 per cent of Vietnamese live in cities and urban areas, the majority live in rural areas. Vietnam's biggest cities are Ho Chi Minh City and Hanoi.

The Kinh (Viet)

The biggest ethnic group in Vietnam is the Kinh (Viet), making up 85 per cent of the population. They began migrating to Vietnam from South China in the 17th century.

Vietnam is also home to 54 minority groups, which make up about 9 million people.

The Tay

Tay are the second largest ethnic group. They mainly live in Northeast Vietnam and their villages are named after nearby mountains and rivers.

The Khmer

About a million Khmer live along the Mekong Delta and maintain their own languages and traditions. They practice either Brahmanism or Buddhism. Their main trades are wet rice cultivation, weaving and pottery.

The Rhade

The Rhade are matriarchal, which means women are the head of the family and families are named after the female elder. Women propose to men and children take their mother's maiden name.

The Hmong

There are around a million Hmong who live in small communities in Northwest Vietnam. Each of the four separate Hmong cultures has its own language.

DAILY LIFE

Family is the foundation of life in Vietnam and it is common for two or more generations to live together. Younger adults are expected to take care of the elderly, while younger grandparents take care of the children. Families are patrilineal, which means that elder family members live and are cared for by their son's wife and children.

Learn the Lingo

Xin chào
Hello

Tôi đói
I'm hungry

Tạm biệt
Goodbye

Tôi khát nước
I'm thirsty

Cám ơn
Thank you

EDUCATION

The Vietnamese value education and Vietnam's education system has advanced along with the country's economic progress. All citizens have a right to an education and it is compulsory to attend school from Grade 1 to Grade 5. Vietnam has a 94 per cent adult literacy rate.

The official language in schools is Vietnamese but the law states that ethnic groups have the right to also learn their own language and writing systems.

Did You Know?

Children in Vietnam go to school six days a week.

LIFE IN CITIES AND RURAL AREAS

Aerial view of Ho Chi Minh City at night

Cities

Vietnam's cities are bursting at the seams with the constant influx of people who move there looking for work. Most people live in apartments, often with many other family members. It's not unusual for three generations of a family to live in one small apartment.

Village Life

Villages in Vietnam vary, depending on location and climate. The Mekong Delta and Ha Long Bay have floating villages. People in the north live in large family compounds, while highland homes are much smaller and usually have thatched roofs. In the south, village homes are often on stilts to lift them above floodwaters. Common features in rural homes include communal living and ancestral altars.

Floating village on Ha Long Bay

Terraced rice field in Lao Cai province

Agriculture

Vietnam's main agricultural districts are the Red River Delta and the Mekong River Delta. Over 37 per cent of Vietnam's workers make their living from agriculture.

Wetland rice farming has traditionally been the main form of agriculture and some parts of the country have two or three rice harvests a year. Vietnam is now the world's second largest rice exporter. This has improved the lives of people in rural areas.

Other important crops include corn, nuts, banana, sugarcane, cassava (manioc), sweet potatoes, coconut and citrus fruits.

Rural Areas

About 65 per cent of Vietnamese people live in rural communities, where the way of life has not changed much for generations. Families still live in traditional style homes and own farms or small businesses.

Water buffalo are calm, helpful animals

Fast Fact

Ploughing is often still done by water buffalo.

RELIGION, FESTIVALS AND HOLIDAYS

The Vietnamese practice six major religions: Buddhism, Catholicism, Protestantism, Islam, Caodaism and Hoa Hao Buddhism.

Around 10 per cent of Vietnamese people practice tam giáo, also known as The Three Teachings. Tam giáo is a combination of Buddhism, Taoism and Confucianism. Around 5 per cent of Vietnamese people practice Christianity and a further 5 per cent practice Caodaism. Nearly half of the population practices some folk religion, while small numbers identify with the indigenous and animistic faiths.

Buddhist monks wear robes that were traditionally coloured using the spice saffron

Buddhism

First introduced into Vietnam during AD 1000, Buddhism is now the most popular religion in Vietnam. There are two main branches of Buddhism: Mahayana and Theravada.

Trang Nguyen – Wandering Souls Day

This festival takes place during the seventh month of the lunar calendar (September). During this time, it is believed that the veil between the spirit world and the human world is lifted. Many families visit their local temples to make offerings, worship their ancestors and clean graves.

Tet Trung Thu

Tet Trung Thu is also known as the Mid-Autumn Festival, Children's Festival or the Harvest Festival. This festival falls on the eighth month of the Lunar calendar (October). Vietnamese people celebrate by making and eating moon cakes and watching special Lion Dance displays.

Tet Trung Thu is celebrated with special foods such as moon cakes

Lion Dance show performed in Ho Chi Minh City.

Tet Nguyen Dan – Lunar New Year

Known simply as Tet, the most important date on the Vietnamese calendar falls in late January or early February, depending on the moon's cycle. It marks the Lunar New Year and the beginning of spring as the Festival of the First Morning of the First Day. Shops are closed and families spend time together.

Thanh Minh – Tomb-sweeping Festival

At the start of the third lunar month (April), families begin cleaning ancestral graves. They make offerings of food, flowers and paper votive objects to show respect to those that have passed.

Hai Ba Trung

The Hai Ba Trung Festival is a special day for women. On the sixth day of March each year, Vietnamese people celebrate the heroic Trung sisters, who led a three-year rebellion against Chinese rule almost 2,000 years ago.

Detail from *The Thirteen Emperors* scroll by Yan Liben (601-673) depicting Emperor Wu (centre)

Chinese Rule

Chinese Emperor Wu of Han conquered Northern Vietnam around 111 BC, beginning nearly 1,000 years of Chinese rule. In AD 40, Vietnam's famous Trung sisters led an unsuccessful three-year rebellion against the Chinese. In AD 939, the Chinese were finally overthrown and the self-proclaimed Emperor, Dinh Bo Linh, officially established Dai Co Viet – the independent state of Vietnam.

Warrior Sisters

Trung Trac and her younger sister, Trung Nhi, are national heroines. They led a revolt against China between AD 40 and AD 39. They were daughters of a powerful lord from the Hanoi area, who launched an army of 80,000 soldiers – many of whom were women – to fight the Han Chinese and drive them out of Vietnam. Although they were eventually defeated by the Chinese, who continued their control for eight more centuries, the legendary courage of the Trung sisters lives on.

The Trung sisters were honoured with large parades

French poster from the 1902 Hanoi world trade fair exhibition

French Colonialism

In 1882, the French attacked Hanoi and took control of the north. By 1859 French colonial rule had begun in South Vietnam. French Indochina, which included Vietnam, Cambodia and Laos, lasted, until 1954.

Ho Chi Minh

Ho Chi Minh was born Nguyen Tat Thank in 1890. He was the president of North Vietnam from 1954 to 1969 and the leader of the movement against French and then American occupation. He was well educated and spent time in Paris as a young man, where he was one of the founding members of the French Communist Party. He spent time in Russia and then China near the Vietnam border, where he helped organise the Vietnam Revolutionary Youth League.

Fast Fact

Cochichina was the name given to the southern region of Vietnam during the French colonial period.

THE VIETNAM WAR AND AFTERWARDS

The Vietnam War was fought between the Communists in the north of Vietnam and the Republicans in the south of Vietnam. Countries that wanted to stop the spread of communism, like the United States and Australia, supported the South.

In 1975, after 20 years of war, the Republican south finally fell to the Communist north. The fall of Saigon (now renamed Ho Chi Minh City) signalled the end of the war. Over 130,000 Vietnamese were evacuated by air and sea, 50,000 of whom formed the largest aerial evacuation in history.

The War Remnants Museum in Ho Chi Minh City explains the American involvement in Vietnam from the Vietnamese perspective

Operation Frequent Wind evacuated American civilians and at-risk Vietnamese from Saigon

The next wave of refugees from Vietnam came on boats and through refugee camps in Southeast Asia. It is impossible to know how many Vietnamese actually fled Vietnam by boat. Sadly many drowned at sea. Between 1975 and 1995, 800,000 boat people arrived safely in countries such as Hong Kong, Indonesia, Malaysia, Thailand, Singapore and the Philippines.

In 1979 the Orderly Departure Program began, making it possible for Vietnamese to migrate directly from Vietnam to other countries. In total, 1.3 million refugees were resettled around the world, including 823,000 in the USA, 19,000 in Britain and 137,000 in both Canada and Australia.

Reunification Palace

This building in Ho Chi Minh City is also known as Independence Palace. This is where the Vietnam War officially ended, when the tanks of North Vietnam crashed through the gates and took control of this government building. It looks just as it did on that day in April 1975.

Reunification Palace in Ho Chi Minh City

China Beach

During the Vietnam War, US troops landed on China Beach near Da Nang in central Vietnam. Over the course of the war, American troops would visit the beach to swim and even surf. This picturesque white sandy beach is now lined with resorts and the bustling city of Da Nang.

Cu Chi Tunnels

Although there are tunnels located all over the country, the most famous are in the Cu Chi area of Ho Chi Minh City. Parts of the tunnel system are now popular tourist attractions and tourists are allowed to enter and see the conditions in the tunnels for themselves. Signs at the entrance warn visitors that anyone with claustrophobia should not enter the tunnels.

Cu Chi tunnels in Ho Chi Minh City

TOP SITES

Ho Chi Minh City

Ho Chi Minh City (HCMC) in the south is Vietnam's largest city, with a population of over 8.8 million. The name was changed after the Vietnam War when the city was merged with the surrounding region, however locals continue to call it Saigon. This chaotic metropolis is often the starting point for visitors to Vietnam.

Hue

Located in central Vietnam, Hue served as the capital of a unified Vietnam between 1802 and 1945. It was also the seat of the Nguyen Dynasty, Vietnam's last ruling family, who held power for 143 years. One of the main attractions of Hue is the Imperial Tombs of the Emperors, where the Nguyen Emperors are buried.

Tomb of Emperor Khai Dinh in Hue

Hanoi

This is Vietnam's second largest city and also its capital. It has a population of about 7.7 million people. Hanoi has been inhabited since around 3000 BC and has been occupied at different times by the Chinese, Japanese, and French. Today, it's a bustling, cosmopolitan city.

Ha Long Bay

Ha Long Bay, located in the north, is a stunning area of limestone pillars and about 1,600 islands covering 1,553 square kilometres. It is a UNESCO World Heritage area and one of Vietnam's most popular tourist destinations. Some areas of the bay are closed to tourism, while others are filled with cruise ships and overnight junk boats.

GEOGRAPHY

Vietnam is an 'S' shaped country. While not large, it is geographically diverse. Vietnam shares borders with Cambodia, Laos and the People's Republic of China. The body of water to the east is the South China Sea.

Golden Valley in Da Lat

Vietnam has 3,260 kilometres of coastline, with the Gulf of Tonkin to the east and the Gulf of Thailand to the south. Only about 20 per cent of the country is level land. The rest is tropical lowlands and densely-forested highlands.

Vietnam is divided into three geographic regions: Bac Bo in the north, Nam Bo in the south and Trung Bo in the central region between them.

Terraced rice field in Mu Cang Chai, near Sapa

Bac Bo – The North

Northern Vietnam is the birthplace of Vietnamese civilisation. The Hoang Lien mountain range overlooks the 7,000 square kilometre Red River Delta and terraced rice fields. The Sapa Valley lies west of Hanoi and Ha Long Bay's 1,600 limestone islands lie to the east.

Trung Bo – Central Region

The Trung Son mountain range dominates Trung Bo and many hill tribes live in this area. It stretches 1,100 kilometres and separates Vietnam from Laos and Cambodia. The region's coastal plains are the location for some of Vietnam's most historical cities, such as Hoi An, Da Nang and Hue, the former imperial city.

Nam O Beach in Da Nang

Mangrove forest in the Can Gio district

Nam Bo – The South

To the south are the fertile plains of the Mekong River, which breaks into nine great tributaries (or nine dragons as the Vietnamese call them) when it reaches Vietnam. The lower part of the Mekong isn't suitable for rice cultivation. Instead its mangrove forests are home to a vast array of birds. To the southwest are mountainous areas known as the highlands, where farmers grow rubber, tea and coffee.

Mighty Mekong

The Mekong is the longest river in Southeast Asia and one of the twelve great rivers of the world. It is 4,350 kilometres long, beginning in Tibet and flowing into the South China Sea.

CLIMATE

Vietnam's three regions have their own climate zones. The North has a cooler season, where winter temperatures drop to a mild average of 17 to 22 degrees. The rest of the year is hot and humid.

South Vietnam lies just above the equator and enjoys a tropical climate all year round. The rainy season is from June to October and the dry season is from November to May.

In the highlands and mountains, temperatures can be quite cool. The central region's climate varies between its north and south, the coastal lowlands and its highlands. Vietnam receives an average of two metres of rain annually.

Flooded streets in Hoi An

Natural Disasters

The country's location and geography makes it vulnerable to natural disasters such as cyclones and other extreme weather events.

TRANSPORT

Traffic queues in Ho Chi Minh city

Driving in Vietnam isn't for the faint of heart. For newcomers to the country, it can appear as if there are no road rules at all. Cycle rickshaw is a popular means of short-distance transport, as are motorbikes. Vietnam's bus network is extensive and cheap.

Vietnam Airlines has a comprehensive domestic network, along with three other domestic airlines. Flying between destinations within Vietnam is cheap and popular. There are also three international airports: Hanoi, Ho Chi Minh and Da Nang.

You can arrive in Vietnam by boat from Cambodia. There are also popular boat trips along the Mekong Delta region. Ha Long Bay in Vietnam's north is a popular cruise region and the bay is busy with overnight junk cruises.

Rail

One of the most popular modes of transport in Vietnam is the train. Vietnamese trains are inexpensive and safe. The Reunification Express joins Ho Chi Minh in the south with Hanoi in the north. Completed by the French in 1936, this 36-hour journey is one of the world's great train rides, along 1,726 kilometres of track.

THE ARTS

Over the centuries, Chinese, Malaysian, Indian and European cultures have influenced Vietnam's arts and crafts, yet they have evolved into distinctly Vietnamese traditions. Woodblock prints and silk paintings are particularly popular.

Craftsman drying traditional mats in Dinh Yen, Dong Thap Province

Dong Ho Village artist creating traditional woodcuts, Quoc Oai district, Hanoi

Many traditional arts can be found in craft villages or small communities, where all the inhabitants are involved in the same trade. Trades include the manufacture of mats, rice wine, knives, bamboo birdcages and ceramics. The old quarter in Hanoi has 36 streets. Each street showcases artisans who specialise in one particular type of service or goods.

Lacquerware

Introduced into Vietnam from China, the art of lacquerware was often handed down from generation to generation. In the early 20th century, the French opened a school to train artists in an effort to meet French demand for lacquerware. Today, there are highly-trained artists, some with a more modern touch.

Lacquerware gifts on sale in Ho Chi Minh City

Literature

Vietnam has a strong oral tradition, meaning that stories and legends were passed down through the generations. Early written works used modified Chinese characters. Arguably the most significant work is the 200-year-old *Tale of Kieu*, an epic poem by Nguyen Du.

Traditional water puppet theatre show in Hanoi

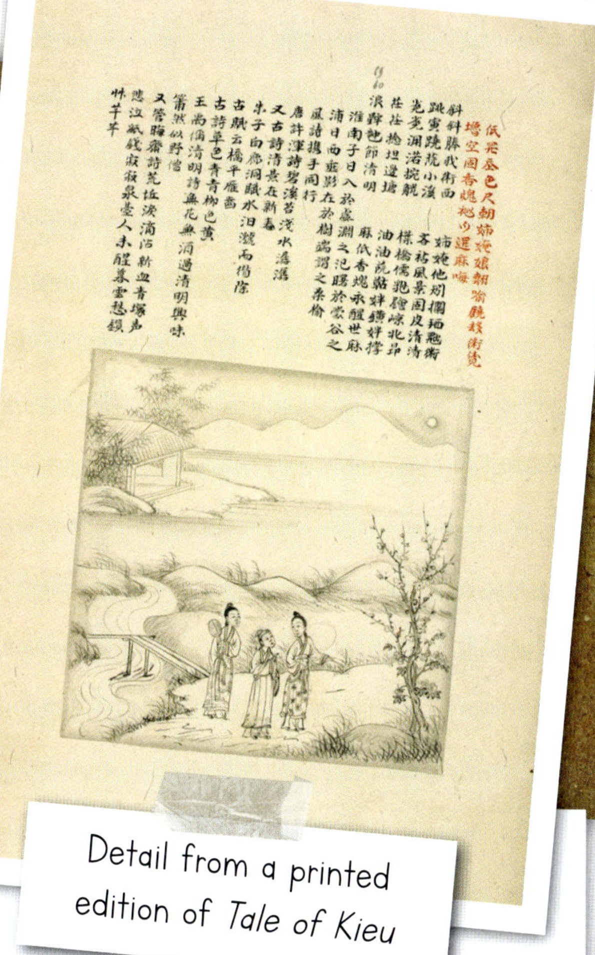

Detail from a printed edition of *Tale of Kieu*

Puppeteers prepare for a performance in Hai Duong

Water Puppetry

The tradition of water puppetry dates back to the 11th century and the Red River Delta area in Northern Vietnam. Wood and lacquer puppets perform over a stage of water, manipulated by puppeteers who sit behind a screen. The themes of the plays performed range from legends, history and folklore to tales passed down about life in rural Vietnam.

FOOD

Mealtime is very important in Vietnam. Traditionally, Vietnamese cuisine is healthy, with taste, fragrance and presentation being important features of a meal.

When designing a meal, one of the considerations is a balance between the five Asian elements of spicy, sour, bitter, salty and sweet. Yin and yang, the combination of two opposite halves which, when combined, complete the whole, are also important. Meals are designed around spiciness and temperature, to create balance in the body.

Family enjoying the Tat Nien meal - a traditional New Year's Eve celebration

While Vietnamese cuisine differs from region to region, what remains consistent is the use of fresh ingredients, including herbs. Steamed rice is a staple food, as are squid and eel. Other meats such as beef, chicken and pork are eaten in smaller amounts.

On the Menu

The national dish of Vietnam is pho (pronounced 'fur').
This noodle soup is mainly eaten at breakfast, and consists of beef or chicken broth, noodles, onions and slivers of chicken, pork or beef.

FLAG, SYMBOLS AND EMBLEMS

Flag Of Vietnam

The state flag of Vietnam was designed in 1940 and has been used officially since 1945. It is a red flag with a gold star in the centre. Yellow represents the Vietnamese people, while red symbolises revolution and blood. The five points of the star are said to stand for the five principal classes in Vietnamese society: intellectuals, farmers, workers, traders and soldiers.

Emblem Of Vietnam

The emblem of Vietnam has a circular red background with a yellow star in the centre, representing the Communist Party, the revolutionary history of the country and its bright future. A cogwheel and crops represent agricultural and industrial labour working in harmony.

National Anthem

Vietnam's national anthem is *Tien Quan Ca* or *The Marching Song*.

National Flower

The lotus, which symbolises health, beauty, commitment, honor and knowledge, is Vietnam's national flower.

GLOSSARY

Buddhism religion based on the teachings of Buddha

claustrophobia fear of tight or enclosed spaces

culture practices, beliefs and customs of a society or people

delta geographical region where a river divides into smaller rivers and empties into a larger body of water

ethnic group people who share a common culture, language and heritage

highlands mountainous or elevated region

Mekong River trans-boundary river in Southeast Asia

plateau large, flat area found in higher regions

refugee person who has been forced to leave their country in order to escape danger

tropical hot, humid climate

INDEX

ARCTIC OCEAN
GREENLAND
(DENMARK)
ALASKA (USA)
CANADA
ICELAND
FAROE ISLANDS
UNITED KINGDOM
IRELAND
FRANCE
NORTH PACIFIC OCEAN
UNITED STATES
NORTH ATLANTIC OCEAN
PORTUGAL
SPAIN
MOROCCO
ALGERIA
CANARY ISLANDS (SPAIN)
MEXICO
THE BAHAMAS
CUBA
JAMAICA
HAITI
BELIZE
GUATEMALA
HONDURAS
EL SALVADOR
NICARAGUA
COSTA RICA
PANAMA
CAPE VERDE
MAURITANIA
MALI
SENEGAL
THE GAMBIA
BURKINA FASO
GUINEA-BISSAU
GUINEA
COTE D'IVOIRE
GHANA
SIERRA LEONE
LIBERIA
NIGERIA
VENEZUELA
GUYANA
SURINAME
FRENCH GUIANA
COLOMBIA
ECUADOR
LINES ISLANDS
PERU
BRAZIL
SOUTH PACIFIC OCEAN
COOK ISLANDS
BOLIVIA
FRENCH POLYNESIA
PARAGUAY
EASTER ISLAND
SOUTH ATLANTIC OCEAN
ST.HELENA
URUGUAY
ARGENTINA
CHILE
TRISTAN DA CUNHA
GOUGH ISLAND
FALKLAND ISLANDS (UK)
SOUTH GEORGIA (UK)